Blue Exhaust

poems by

Janet Reed

Finishing Line Press
Georgetown, Kentucky

Blue Exhaust

*for Anne,
first editor,
first reader,
first believer*

Copyright © 2019 by Janet Reed
ISBN 978-1-63534-891-0 First Edition
All rights reserved under International and Pan-American Copyright Conventions. No part of this book may be reproduced in any manner whatsoever without written permission from the publisher, except in the case of brief quotations embodied in critical articles and reviews.

ACKNOWLEDGMENTS

"Blue Exhaust" and "Broken Nose"—*I-70 Review*
"The Bookmobile"—*River City Poetry*
"Elegy to the Saturday Car Wish"—*The Nassau Review*
"Engine Crisis"—*Crab Creek Review*
"Essay Contest: Spring Open House"—*Sow's Ear Review*
"Frankenstein's Monster"—*The Writer's Café Magazine*
"Heart Attack" and "Revelation 21:8"—*Abbreviate Journal*
"I am not the Same"—*99 Pine Street*
"Intersection of Folly and Aching Need" and "Foreclosure"—*Burning House Press*
"Into the Night Through Open Windows"—*The Laurel Review*
"Looking Back"—*Chiron Review*
"My Dad Speaks of His Father's Death"—*Burningword Literary Journal*
"Our Sister, Mary Magdalene" and "New Clothes"—*the Same*
"Rosemary's Beauty Shop"—*Tipton Poetry Journal*
"Scars"—*The MOON Magazine*
"The Streaker"—*Tell-Tale Inklings*
"Toughs: An Elegy to Third Grade"—*Common Ground Review*
"The Unfixables: Dad and His Red Corvair"—*riverbabble*
"Salvation, 1964;" and "No Coloreds: Sinclair Station, Missouri, 1968"—*Tipton Literary Journal*

Publisher: Leah Maines
Editor: Christen Kincaid
Cover Art: Tia Lynn Nelson
Author Photo: Robin Mooney
Cover Design: Leah Huete

Printed in the USA on acid-free paper.
Order online: www.finishinglinepress.com
also available on amazon.com

Author inquiries and mail orders:
Finishing Line Press
P. O. Box 1626
Georgetown, Kentucky 40324
U. S. A.

Table of Contents

Salvation, 1964 1

Blue Exhaust, April 4, 1668 2

The Coup 3

Revelation 21:8 4

Rosemary's Beauty Shop 5

Toughs: An Elegy to Third Grade 6

Broken Nose, 1968 7

Violin Lessons 9

Essay Contest: Spring Open House, April 1968 10

"Win With Wallace in '68" 11

"No Coloreds"—Sinclair Station, Springfield, Missouri, 1968 ...12

So Much Depends on Two Wheels and Fireflies 13

Hindsight 14

The Intersection of Folly and Aching Need 15

The Bookmobile 16

My Dad Speaks of His Father's Death 18

The Unfixables: Dad and His Red Corvair 20

Elegy to the Saturday Car Wash 21

Engine Crisis 22

Our Sister, Mary Magdalene 23

Into the Night Through Open Windows 24

The Streaker 25

Looking Back 26

Heart Attack 27

I am not the Same 28

Foreclosure 29

Frankenstein's Monster 30

Frames of Motherhood 31

New Clothes 33

Sock Widow Empathy 34

Scar Tissue 35

Salvation, 1964

> *Yet knowing how way leads on to way, I doubted if I should ever come back.*
> *Robert Frost*

My father succumbed to salvation
one Wednesday night two years
after my mother fell in love
with *thou-shalt-not*
shouted by a preacher
so taken with Leviticus
his *a-BOM-in-A-shuns*
hissed and hung in the air
like a lit fuse ready to blow
the lakes of hell into a blaze of brimstone.

Had dad's love of fast cars
and finely-tuned engines held
through my mother's zeal,
if he'd found enough synergy
in stock car pit crews
and Goodyear tire checks
to silence the snake charmers
he might have evaded the Call
until my mother fell in love with Avon calling.

Instead, he took to that Black Book
like his father took to whiskey,
slurring sin like gin straight up,
preaching the wages of death
in the depths of his heart's hell
the cries of the damned on his lips
the gnashing of teeth his own,
fury flashing faster than a crashed car
on a Daytona wall.

I was pinned inside, his passenger
on a fast track to collision,
held past bedtime, past the news at ten,
quoting his Book King James perfect—
lambs and goats, devils and angels,
then released to dream his fire,
my small body consumed by heat.

Blue Exhaust
April 4, 1968

At eight, sunk in the back seat
of my dad's red Corvair, yawning
into my pink flannels, I lost faith fast,
the way a bandage ripped from skin
tears the weave of wound it's tended.

The night of the Murder in Memphis,
we waited in the graveled drive
of a trailer park, car engine idling
waiting for my mother.
The car's engine idled;
my dad slumped in his seat,
hand on the Delco's AM dial,
hummed a hymn with Loretta Lynn.

I still hear their song, still hear
the motor's measured piston taps,
a hollow slap against the stick in park,
still feel the throttle inhale,
a half-beat of syncopation
in an engine once rebuilt
and *still unsafe at any speed.*

Like the whine of a diesel low on oil,
my dad's voice rose as news broke
from Memphis on that AM radio.
His slurs stuttered, then steamed
the windows, a centrifugal force
of words hot enough to break the block,
and still my mother did not come.

Not daring to breathe, my eyes
fixed on the moths kissing yellow bulbs
over the doors of those doublewides,
the oily lights blurring a moving darkness
I did not yet understand, and I choked
on the blue smoke of his exhaust.

The Coup

Unaware of being watched,
I forged my city of sand
with pail and shovel, my town
of Hotwheels expanding
with each toy extracted
from my child's box.
An ambulance needs a hospital,
a bus a school. A race car
without a track cannot compete;
a station wagon stays shiftless
without a house and drive.
My make-believe metropolis
became an unzoned
tangled-traffic mess
that June day long ago
I abandoned it for a drink
only to return and find
my town of toys
the victim of a coup,
a gold and brown
diamond-backed copperhead
coiled around school and home
daring me to call an ambulance.

Revelation 21:8
> *All liars, shall have their part in the lake which burneth with fire and brimstone, which is the second death.*

I learned to count by twenty-fives,
when I was six and denied
knowledge of jelly beans
missing from my mother's bowl
despite Sour Cherry licking
my fingers red, the hues of
Green Apple and Banana Boat
clowning my lips and tongue.
I loved those jelly beans,
all the but the black ones.
Licorice, like Infidels, I left behind.
Liars, my mom said, go to hell
where they burn in great fires.

> *You won't like it there.*

I never forgot about lying
or ever again savored even
my favorite Orange Cream—
too much sick of sin
after penning my penance.
Twenty-five lines per page,
ten pages spread across my room
the lake of fire, my second death,
first making friction, then a spark,
finally a flame—reds and oranges
a conflagration consuming and choking,
the black smoke of this memory,
always separate from my sin.

Rosemary's Beauty Shop

The bright pink smock locked
tight with translucent buttons
announced her trade.
She wore a Beehive
and practiced the backcomb
on wig-ladened heads scattered
at stations around her shop.

Her name was Rosemary;
she heard my mother's confession
at ten on Saturdays while I sat
in the pew of the penitents:
a long row of dryer chairs
with their glass-heavy heads
blowing the hot air of salvation
on those prepared to receive it.

I watched baptismal rituals
at shampoo bowls with salves
and soaps for sins and scalps
left untouched Sabbath to Sabbath.
Church on Sunday was the reason
for Rosemary's on Saturday,
a clean head equal to a clean heart.

This was the creation story
I never knew until blow dryers
replaced backcombs:
six days of bobby pins
and sponge rollers, orange
juice cans and hair nets, one,
the seventh, to rinse and rest.

Redemption for my mother
was a $3.00 ritual of renewal,
repentance and confession
completed when Rosemary
returned her picks and combs
to the glass jar of Barbicide,
emerged from the haze of Aqua Net,
like Jesus descending the mountain
and wrote my mother down
in her book for ten next Saturday.

Toughs: A Pantoum to Third Grade

The sharpener's metal teeth ate our yellow number twos
faster than the gum we outed from our pencil boxes; we
popped its bubbled pink masking the fountain's sour stink
stale in its metal belly as our bellies belched fresh fear.

Faster than the gum we outed from our pencil boxes
we ate each other quicker than our plate lunches
stale in their pot bellies, our bellies belching fresh fear—
survivors, all fits and fists, brawl and brawn, taunts and tics.

We ate each other quicker than our plate lunches,
toughs locked in the teachers closet at recess
survivors of fits and fists, brawl and brawn, taunts and tics
stuffed between unused stacks of *Dick and Jane*

those bad toughs locked in the teacher's closet at recess
lambs baptized in the blood of the playground, bloodied
in the stuffy silence of unused stacks of *Dick and Jane*
Spot, ball, run, play, words we knew but did not know.

Broken Nose, 1968

I rode a second of lightning to blackness
one sunny afternoon in third grade

when Rusty McNeeley's rock missed
Danny Baker's nose, crushing mine instead,

a move that marked me with an "x"—
broad stripes of white tape across my face,

a tic-tac-toe square holding its advantage
for six weeks against the next move

Rusty never made. My mother wanted
an apology, I wanted what I couldn't have—

the moment back before stepping inside
that fight. Even now when the wind

whistles through a car window
at highway speed, or catches the last flutters

of fall leaves clinging to brittle limbs,
I hear an object harder than bone

dance with gravity, feel the burn of impact
as I fall into the grit of the playground,

blood staining sand and two small hands,
waking to the smell of white,

white sheets, walls, a white curtain
keeping me from a boy grieving his loss,

a leg above the knee, his wail full glottal;
hard stops punctured by pain, he was prey

in the teeth of his killer. Caught in the hardest loss
I had ever known, I retched into the whiteness,

ether and fear too strong for a girl wearing
her first Mark of Cain, a low card in a game

of chance trumped by a straight of circumstance.
Today, when I run my hand over old scars,

I think about the legless boy, wonder how
he grew his altered world, and especially think

about Rusty, that red-faced, rock-throwing boy,
wonder if he ever shuddered

playing Rock, Paper, Scissors, if
rock, rock, rock ever ricocheted in his head,

ever broke him wide open in the hard place
a stone makes in a room of loss.

Violin Lessons

If I had to choose, I'd play Bach
or Chopin, a sonata or nocturne.

I didn't know then, ten and eager,
invited to be in the band.

I wanted a sax, flute, silver or gold
bodies shining on ivory buttons,

not strings stretched taut
over bridges dependent on bows

that screeched strings like hawks
or honked like geese in flight.

I craved the smooth touch of a tuba
through white gloves, ached for buttoned

spats crisping the long line of my marching
band pants. Instead, mom handed me

a black case dulled by lost intentions,
said that to take music, I *would take*

her violin, play as she once had,
I, the rib of her instrument.

Our fiddle feud hit all the right notes
in our undoing.

Maybe *Sonata No. 9*, the piece I loved,
the one she hated, traveled train-like

on bad tracks of years past, or maybe
clamped vise-like to her Virginia Reel.

I didn't ask, just put the case away
knowing our keys would always clash.

Essay Contest, Spring Open House, April 1968

> *I came to the conclusion that there is an existential moment in your life when you must decide to speak for yourself; nobody else can speak for you.*
> Martin Luther King, Jr.

Blank lines on primary paper swimming
in my eyes, I fiddled my yellow number two

through hair and fingers until words
came clear—my dad's the night of the Murder

in Memphis, his high praise for a two-bit
jailbird, a white sniper's shotgun spine

splattering black blood on motel cement,
a bullet twisted through the barrel

of a thirty-ought-six, the silencer of dreams.
I didn't know yet how to use words I made

myself, did not know how fear takes aim
at soft targets, but the night my first-place essay

hung outside the door to third grade, I learned
words have fists strong enough for knock-out

blows, that throwing a punch can break a fist.
My essay's blue ribbon invited all the moms and kids

to read words I knew by heart, words not my own,
words that caused my mother to blush and rush away

not stopping to ask if I'd been good
or done my work, not pausing when my teacher

her voice smooth and sweet as meringue
melting on a warm tongue called to our backs:

"Oh, do come back and see the rest;
there's so much more to read."

"Win With Wallace in '68:" George Wallace Campaigns for President in Springfield, Missouri

You've got to be taught before it's too late,
Before you are six or seven or eight,
To hate all the people your relatives hate,
You've got to be carefully taught! South Pacific

At the rally in our hometown,
his *pointy-headed intellectuals*
and *sissy-britches welfare people*
released such scorn in the crowd
the air snorted, feet stamped
like rodeo bulls ready to run.
I stomped, too.

It was a time of revolution,
the summer of love
for *acid-tripping hippies*
but not for my mother,
prim in her white gloves.
Years past signs of separation
leaving gray squares on green walls,
she avoided public restrooms,
refused to let me drink
at water fountains. I was eight.
I didn't argue.

Segregation she said was fairness,
letting brown-skinned kids
learn in their own schools,
swim in their own pools,
pee in their own toilets,
and so we shouted
on the square with other white people:
Segregation Now! Segregation Forever!
For Fairness.

"No Coloreds"—Sinclair Station, Springfield, Missouri, 1968

Until I saw a girl like me denied her right to pee,
I didn't notice water fountains dueling in public places
despite the absence of words
in unpainted squares on walls above them.
I never asked why bathroom keys
hung on pegs behind counters
or why the water fountain words
moved to cardboard, hand lettered,
behind plated glass. I was eight and white.

So small in her dad's backseat,
I would have missed her
had the silence of nothing
in the expectation of something—
a bell at the pump, the cutting of an engine,
the call to *fill 'er up and check the oil*—
been answered. She was strangely still,
no running for the red chest of cold colas
begging for dimes, no head bobbing
out an open car window, bubble gum
popping on her cheeks,
just a silhouette of a girl hazy
in the shadow of afternoon sun.

In the waiting silence, the hired man,
stiff as his uniform stayed still
under the station's sign of service
promised with a smile;
he, mute, as if he did not hear
the bell, did not see the blue Chevy,
did not flinch when the man
untethered long legs and lumbered
toward him, nodding back at his girl.
Pointing only to the sign,
to those old water fountain words,
he told the girl and her dad to drive away
the key dangling untouched on the wall.

So Much Depends on Two Wheels and Fireflies
After William Carlos Williams

When I was ten and a catcher of fireflies I was so
certain my captives in Mason jars prayed as much
for daylight as a kid with a bike and time depends
on freedom to roam, I let my winged friends go on
a whim knowing they'd be back to play. Mornings, a
banana seat between my legs, riding through red
clay, Missouri mud spattering spokes, one wheel
then the other running puddles, jumping a barrow
or two, I rode until the desire to sip a Slurpee glazed
with the sweat of dirty hands led back to the store with
nickel candy, paperbacks, and vats of cherry cola ice raining
sweet in a paper cup. Outside, I scraped water
and wax into its bent rim, a cataract dripping beside
the bike and me sprawled under a tree spent like the
jarred fireflies, a new Nancy Drew in hand, its white
pages dropping eggs of clues in nests of chickens.

Hindsight

> *You can't always get what you want, but if you try sometime,*
> *you'll find you get what you need.*
> Mick Jagger and Keith Richards

My mother collected children like spare tires
tucked into the tire wells of her heart.

Kids rotated in and out of her care faster
than retreads blow on hot highways.

Foster babies, a home for orphans,
neighbors' kids, two adoptees, each

new child promised checkered flags,
a sheen of satisfaction spurred by the steam

of boiling bottles and Saturday night baths
hopped up on boxes of Mr. Bubble.

I was hers, the common denominator
in a factoring of faces, confused by the comings

and especially the goings. I watched her
nurse switchbacks and swerve for strays

only to reverse course in hairpin turns leaving
disappointment bundled like bindles in ditches.

None of us worked out as she wanted, but
seeing her shift through little people as easily

as moving the gear stick from second to third,
I saw what I needed to go the distance:

all-weather wheels, steel-belted, well-warrantied.

The Intersection of Folly and Aching Need

I had no more than left the hollow of her arm,
when she traded in our Chevy
for a Ford wagon and ten kids
living in a home for the motherless,
as if adding the power of ten

to lunch boxes and laundry baskets
could build a ladder
long enough to touch
the bottom of a wordless well.

I was glad when the orphans failed her
as I had failed,
glad to go home, I young enough
to divide only by two:
before and after,
normal and not. I didn't see them

coming, the babies, two
fledglings whose secrets
lay buried in locked drawers,
blank pages of boys
leaving hospital doors
swaddled in her aching need.

Why I stayed quiet past road signs
suggesting exits and turn-abouts
for truth telling, I can't say even now,
but I sat in her backseat through years
of moonlit drives in fantasy lands,
they believing her stories,
seeds inside her womb,
I questioning what I knew was true.

Her hands firm on wheel and map,
she drove us deeper into the night,
time a suspension bridge
between then and now.
When exposure came,
she looked for me, the first born,
behind the wheel of a new Prius
driving off the edge of her map.

The Bookmobile

I read by flashlight,
made blankets of print,
fell asleep on quiet streets
far from our house of lunar eclipse,
where the Good Book fueled darkness,
and Father, broken son
of a broken small-town drunk,
cudgeled compliance,
where Mother, Beehive haloed stiff,
whined *never enough*.

My secret saved me, those books
borrowed on Thursdays after school—
the bookmobile, its sweet-sour
exhaust of machine oil
and chocolate soft serve
called me to the wild things
in the belly of the bus:
hobbit holes, wardrobe portals,
blue-backed bios,
Nathan Hale, Boy Patriot,
Amelia waving good-bye from her cockpit.

Banned cargo stowed in my bag,
I pedaled my Schwinn home,
a racer making up lost time,
to squeeze past Father walking
the floor to the whine of steel guitars,
his home-built hi-end hi-fi
the devil's backbone dropping
drink and redneck failure 'til dinner—
to rock by Mother in the kitchen
spinning her blue-suede Elvis
love me tender tracks
from a mouth pale with aching needs,

to hide my contraband under sheets,
where after devotionals, I would
spin webs with spiders,
find clues in old clocks,
fly the skies with heroes,

then dream of railway stations,
first-class tickets to places I would go,
and blank pages of adventures I would write.

My Dad Speaks of His Father's Death

When dad's grief
unbottled itself,
when he could not square

his guilt over the dad
he could not love,
when his beast of a past

coiled him, a rattler
ready to strike,
he would tell the story.

I still try to picture it,
my grandfather,
deep lines in his red face,

trademark overalls,
a Fedora tipped
over one eye,

ordering a whiskey
from a line of bottles
behind bored barkeeps,

the bar's stale gloom,
barely visible through
the smoke of Camels

fingered by old drinkers
schlumped on stools,
regulars like him

who wished he'd
get on with it, shoot
the bitch and bastard,

or shut the fuck up.
No one this night noticed
how his pocket curved,

saw his old Army pistol,
a loaded Colt .45,
that minutes later

just outside their reach
would bare
its yellow heat

into the bar's plate
glass, didn't guess
how whiskey still

in hand, he'd smoke
the orange circles
of streetlights

and red neons
flashing nickel beer
and Budweiser,

or how bar mirrors
would reflect a man
slurried in a slough

of his own making
melt down on a
cracked sidewalk,

alone with the years
that tripped
him there,

his boy left behind,
frozen in time
no feeling in his blue feet.

The Unfixables: Dad and His Red Corvair

His lady, a red kiss along the white teeth
of bucket seats, sat as dad did on Sundays

in the shelter of a steeple, the car sunkissed
spotless inside its blacktopped lines, he,

white shirt starched stiff as his pew, Black Book
spread across his legs, asking for all that eluded him.

My dad loved that beauty the way I wanted
him to love us, the way I now wish he'd loved

himself, more than a stuttering engine
that fell from grace faster than penitents

at a tent meeting after the singing. His was
an engine in crisis; parts parted and prayed over,

oily fingers smudging the pages of his motor manual
as rods and pistons grappled for attention,

their stoplight coughs of blue exhaust filming
the sheen of that red baby, stains he washed away

before church each week when wrist deep
in Turtle Wax, he made its soiled skin shimmer

like scarlet sin in a Sunday hymn, asking only
Who Will Pray for Me, Fallen Angel?

Elegy to the Saturday Car Wash

My dad knew his way around the curves
of fenders and creases of tail lights
as he readied the car and himself
on Saturdays for church on Sundays,
the shade of two front-yard Elms his automat.
Chamois in hand, he bent into the crevices
as if a single streak of tar marred
his sense of self, proved he was a man
unworthy of the name.

The son of a town drunk famous for failure,
my dad made cleanliness the litmus for rightness
his surrogate for nights left in pickups
outside country bars, for guns held
to a ten-year-old's head in the dead of night,
those old bruises still wickedly purple.
A loaded gun himself, he wrestled
like Jacob to make sense of things,
exhausted his demons in the greens
of Turtle Wax and Mr. Clean.

Road grunge and baked on bugs washed away,
he let the sagging web of his aluminum chair
bear the weight of his silent thoughts.
While shafts of light filtered fading shadows,
haloed the bright red body of his main lady,
the redneck hymns of Johnny and Porter
moved him for a moment from
Ring of Fire to A Satisfied Mind.

Engine Crisis

Spent parts littered his garage floor:
camshaft, carburetor, and clamps.
Hoses bled out their old clots,
and molted belts snaked
the gray concrete.

My dad was rebuilding
the car's engine as he rebuilt
himself when things
went wrong like teeth
grinding gears and groins
to such unholy messes
not even Johnny Cash's
Boy Named Sue, his hymn
and hero, could spit
penance on broken pieces.

I hugged my knees to a chest
still flat as checkers
and watched my dad
torque and twist,
then push and pull
as if life were on the line.
When his crescent wrench
clattered on the concrete,
he wiped barber-striped grease
from his cheek, walked down
the drive and out of sight,
Cash still spilling heartbreak
through the speakers of his GE radio.

Our Sister, Mary Magdalene

In the Age of Aquarius, girls shed
ratted Beehives and bouffants

for long straight hair; they ditched
A-line dresses for short skirts

and white go-go boots, but at steepled
doors, old men stood guard with yardsticks

measuring skin above the boot,
covered knees a girl's price of prayer.

Those of us too young for the yardstick
watched our sisters shamed

and shared their blame for the wet,
dark place of our sex, for hips of white bone

framing the purse of eggs we carried,
too easily opened, and we

the sole bearers of Eve's curse
when it did, bloodied, we our brothers' ribs,

always the Mary Magdalene sought
with hard breaths under the moon,

denied in daylight, our names
soiled and spit like devil's venom.

Into the Night Through Open Windows
Butterflies are free to fly, fly away, high away, bye, bye.
Elton John

On the nights I blew the smoke
of Virginia Slims at the moon,
I wished it would choke the men
who thought they owned it.
Those nights I slipped through
open windows, I found my Jesus
in fruit jars juiced red
with Strawberry Hill,
swooning under the orange haze
of dappled lights in empty lots
to Elton on eight-tracks.
The hook of a riff, a lick of longing,
the taste of too-sweet booze,
and a long drag of *you've come*
a long way, baby, lifted me
from my Father's house.
I was sixteen,
carousing with strangers,
leaning into open car windows,
singing my hymn of praise:
someone saved my life tonight.

The Streaker

My parents loathed the college:
*It crawls with longhaired
hippie smokers and draft dodgers*

too much like ants on a picnic march
to baskets of ham salad and deviled eggs.

Once during a football game,
a streaker in white Converses
danced the full monty
under stadium lights,
swung in the breeze of a fall night
and laughed at the rules of the game.

Eager for a public shaming,
my parents drove to the crime scene:
the streaker's touchdown,
the play-by-play
run and manhunt
breaking news on the car's radio.

This was the night my dad said:
education never done nobody no good,
the night I learned ants
would always find lunch,
clothing was optional,
and that white Converses
would carry me into stadium lights
and touchdowns of the mind.

Looking Back

> *Yet in my heart I will never deny her, who suffered death because she chose to turn.*
> *Anna Akhmatova*

I hit the highway out of town at eighteen
three years past my mind's exit sign,
on the day Elvis died, never to look back—
leaving the house of sand and salt,
opposite ends of a moral compass,
the future a sweet lady
of aces and double sevens.

I left the interstate too soon. It was night,
and wild deer leaped between the crags
and into both lanes of state highways,
their eyes green in my headlights.
Somewhere in Arkansas, not Hope
but Searcy, my Datsun broke down.
It was Sunday, near a Church, its lights
bright against a starless sky,
its members singing a siren song
of rescue I knew and I began to hum.

Losing the past proved as plausible
as a suspect staying cool under
jaundiced bulbs of interrogation.
I stammered explanations,
faltered singing hymns
I'd known all my life, but I let the saints
fix my truck and send me home.
It was the first but not the last time
I would look back, rewind the exit,
certain this time I knew where to turn.

Heart Attack

    In her wheelchair,
she reminded me of Imelda Marcos,
the First Lady of Exorbitance,
receiving another pair of shoes
from a dutiful supplicant.
Fiddling with the Bazooka-pink bows
on her nightgown, shuffling her
Dollar Store slippers on and off
the footrests, she watched
while I fumbled with the green cylinder
and pliable tubing
the pressure and prayer
releasing us from her bed of stinks—
sour sponge and deep funk.
"You have a lot to learn,"
she declaimed as the valve
hissed and burped
its metered time.
We headed toward
any- distraction- will- do,
she twisting her IV'd wrist
into a queen's wave
at each passing nurses' station.
These weekend rituals
pleased enough. Enough—
the thing most hoped for,
the evidence not likely seen in the
blunder, blame, and disappointment
I understood as our recursive theme.
Being her air had made me dizzy.
She wasn't the first of us, after all,
to have survived a heart attack.

I am not the Same

I know we can't know what we don't. I'm not proud of what I thought I knew and didn't. *Go* and *for keeps* made no sense. The Grim Reaper had rapped often enough on her door and been turned away: "I'm not opening that door, young man," she'd say, "you go visit someone else today." Once, on the gurney and prepped for surgery, hair netted, IV dripping, a smile tickling the corners of her mouth, she crooned: "Maybe we better hold off and think this through." Her hip was in pieces. She was too much like Amanda Wingfield flying over Blue Mountain jonquils clasped to her breast in that moment. Frustrated by obstinacy, surrounded by obligations unsympathetic to red blood cell counts and systolic pressures, I stamped my foot with the immediacy of now. "I'm not dying today," she countered. And she didn't. Months earlier, blending boiling soup, I burned my arm. The blister had oozed and wept while I slept next to her hospital bed, and I was scared. You understand, don't you? Orphans *are* born at 52. I am a fossil in times of crisis. Or maybe a wild lioness circling and waiting to run. I was present when the Reaper knocked the last time, and I am not the same. There was before. There was after. *I am not the same.*

Foreclosure

Her alligator appetites had long devoured
the marshes, owned the bayous
in the rooms of our house

by the time she was widowed at sixty.
Our live- in- the- moment mother
trained us to feed on each other,

three kids circling the rope-ringed
dining room while she preened
and called the play-by-plays.

She was our Suffering Jesus, her
pale mouth of aching needs
silenced all but the grandfather clock.

I saw its big hand cross the small one,
stall at six, and I became
the clock winder staving off

mortgage meltdowns, fractures
too fine to fix. She scoffed
she'd be dead when the bank

took the house, blamed Father
for holes in the walls and binged
on leather minis, three-inch heels,

leopard prints and push-up bras;
she starved herself sick, her body
her eighteen-year-old self reincarnate,

the last of my red-lettered tantrums,
I a daughter unable to compete
with such a mother, I quit keeping

her time. When she died,
my foretelling hit like pocket change
dropped recklessly on the nightstand.

We kids retreated to silent corners,
nothing to save, and on the steps
of the courthouse, the hammer nailed *sold*.

Frankenstein's Monster

> *When falsehood can look so like the truth, who can assure themselves of certain happiness?*
> Mary Shelley, *Frankenstein*

My brother kicks at stones,
wanders the night streets
blowing breath on bluing fingers,
looking for a warm place
to stay the night.
Before he knew
she was not his mother,
he was her creature.
Now, he dumpster digs
for crackers and Hi-Hos,
swallows uppers he begs,
asks rooms of strangers.
He is Clyde without Bonnie,
his sass and piss silent
in the cold, his past
hiding like pocket lint
rubbing against numb fingers.
I wait for word he fell or froze,
no blanketed box, no doorway.
Comforted by a coat of ocean mist,
he is no longer cast off no longer lost.

Frames of Motherhood
> *A beautiful thing never gives so much pain as does failing to see and hear it.*
> *Michelangelo*

My tour guide weaves through the multitudes
in these Vatican galleries so nimbly
I've lost sight of her though her voice
still whispers must-not-miss details in my ear.
I'm not listening, these pictures of the Virgin
and her baby hold nothing for me, my
motherhood frames hundreds of miles
and a lifetime away in the shale
and red clay of my Missouri roots
where the moms and babies I knew
often went missing from each other's lives.

No painting of Jesus or his mother ever
moved me more than the mom and kids
I met one Christmas Eve, they in need of a room
on the holiest night of the year, one when snow
drifted along the fencerows and frost thickened
the inside of our old farmhouse, a home
for the motherless, large enough
for the twelve of us,
little disciples clean and eager
to open the gifts of strangers,
Church ladies busy since June,
the standard orphan fare:
knitted scarves and hats, children's Bibles,
No-Tears Shampoo, and Mr. Bubble boxes.

This night, Bobby Hodge, the oldest of us,
bragged his *real* mom sent presents,
and Billy Bryant whose mom did not
sneered they wouldn't be good ones,
that the one who dumped Bobby in this place
was *one mean somuvabitch,*
a comment Billy paid for with the frown
of our housemom and a pocked bar
of soap pushed through his lips.

I was five, the first to answer the knock,
And now I stand here in this gallery
wondering what he would have painted,
Raphael, if he stood with me looking
at faces warmed by cups of cocoa,
and colored ribbons, or out at the shivering four,
a madonna and three babes,
the snow on their coats
thick as the fur matted on their collars,
she presenting her gold at a warm manger.

Could Caravaggio in all his Medusa madness
capture the darkness on their receding backs
when our housemom,
satisfied with the suds on Billy's teeth
stepped in to say we had no room,
rules being rules?

So far from these Vatican frames, their ideals
of motherhood, of a woman who never asked
to mother but loved her boy to his death
in spite of it. Instead, I see
the lace of ice tatting taller on glass panes
the night our housemom
turned away little children
without so much as a cup of cocoa,
then offered up the gifts of strangers.

New Clothes

Those old things crammed in corners
shouted their accusations;

pant legs dangled on hangers,
sweaters swallowed shelves, self-righteous

in their refusal to fit, obstinate
in not giving an inch or half:

black and white capris
checkered like a raceway flag

white no-iron Oxford button-ups
Catholic school-girl stiff and prim

tees that whined about the stretch,
bras and belts that wouldn't hook.

I loved how I once looked in them:
Friday casual, chic couture—

many faces of Eve in threaded cottons
silks and linen, polyester blends.

I may not have shed myself as intended
but I slipped the skin of chameleons

sloughed the waist of conformity,
lost the buttons of silence.

New clothes hang in this girl's closet,
and she can breathe inside their elastic bands.

Sock Widow Empathy

Empathy happens
when you do your laundry,
finally folding socks
bottom feeding in the basket
and discover your favorites

became widows
in the wash cycle,
and you mourn
their alien aloneness—
pairs without partners.

It happens
when you are waiting
in a long line of cars,
and a sound breaks through
the idling engines:

geese—a whole family
honking their goose joy
with such ardor you
forget about the old man
holding up the line.

Or, when you call a road-
trip to escape your past
and find your face always
in the rearview mirror
the past in the present.

That's when you know
the ache to be part of more
than you and you know
why erasers need pencils,
why words are fire.

Scar Tissue

> *The world breaks everyone, and afterward*
> *some are strong at the broken places.*
> *Hemingway*

Before a scar
    is a sudden split of skin

a too-ripe melon
    popped open, jagged

its body unable to contain it,
    seeds and rind splattering

walls and floor,
    its meat juicing and clotting

before pain
    consumes it,

salt that burns flesh
    until the scab sloughs

showing the weave of a basket
    in the brokenness

the close of the raw,
    the holder of grief—

latticework that promises
    nothing will ever

hurt so bad
    in that place again.

Janet Reed was born and still resides in Missouri. She travels widely and reads voraciously to mix the culture of the Midwest with impressions of global identity. She began writing stories on wide-lined notebook paper when she was eleven, and after earning a Master's degree from Pittsburgh State University and teaching writing and literature for the better part of 20 years, she began publishing creative work. She has been nominated twice for a Pushcart Prize and for Best of the Web. Her work has appeared in multiple journals. She currently teaches at Crowder College. *Blue Exhaust* is her first book.

www.ingramcontent.com/pod-product-compliance
Lightning Source LLC
LaVergne TN
LVHW041552070426
835507LV00011B/1054